Baby Sign Language

Made Easy Guide for Early and Easy Communication Through Sign Before Your Baby Can Talk

Barbara S. Johnson

Copyright © 2020 Barbara S. Johnson

All rights reserved. No part of this publication may be reproduced, distributed, or transmitted in any form or by any means, including photocopying, recording, or other electronic or mechanical methods, without the prior written permission of the publisher, except in the case of brief quotations embodied in critical reviews and specific other non-commercial uses permitted by copyright law.

Table of Contents

BABY SIGN LANGUAGE 1

INTRODUCTION 5

CHAPTER 1 8
- OVERVIEW OF SIGN LANGUAGE 8
  - *Why it could be neither helpful nor dangerous* 10
  - *Learning baby sign* 13

CHAPTER 2 20
- TRAINING YOUR BABY SIGN LANGUAGE 20
  - *Starting out* 20
  - *Baby sign language* 21
  - *Is Your Son Or Daughter Ready?* 21
  - *Inspiration* 23

CHAPTER 3 24
- SIGN LANGUAGE FOR INFANTS 24
  - *Start Speaking* 24

CHAPTER 4 27
- TEACH YOUR CHILD SIGN LANGUAGE 27
  - *Caregivers* 27

CHAPTER 5 30
- LEARN BABY CHAT SIGN LANGUAGE 30
  - *Sign Mixtures* 30
  - *Linking the area* 32

CHAPTER 6 34
- BABY SIGN LANGUAGE TECHNIQUES 34
- TONING DOWN STRESS 34

CHAPTER 7 37
- TRAIN YOUR CHILD SIGN LANGUAGE 1 37

Advancing *37*

CHAPTER 8 ....**41**

Advance Toddler Sign Language 2 41

Your Developing Child *41*

CHAPTER 9 ....**45**

Teaching Infants Sign Language 45

Obtaining More Signers *45*

Infant's sign language *45*

CHAPTER 10 ....**47**

What to Do When Things do not go as Planned 47

CHAPTER 11 ....**50**

More Signs and Indicators 50

CONCLUSION **53**

ACKNOWLEDGMENTS **57**

INTRODUCTION

A fresh new beginner's guide to American Sign Language!

Baby Sign Language Simplified book makes it fun and straightforward to communicate with your child long before they can talk.

From clapping their hands in excitement to lifting their arms to be carried, babies are naturally inclined to use gestures to communicate. With *Baby Sign Language Simplified*, you'll discover useful, everyday signs that will help you understand what your child is saying while having fun and strengthening your bond simultaneously.

Long before they can talk, babies have a whole lot to say. With this adorable book of vital signs, babies and parents can quickly learn how to communicate their needs, wants, and feelings and even make necessary observations with a simple gesture. Studies show that babies who use sign language feel less frustrated, throw fewer tantrums, and often learn to talk more easily.

This book delivers the step-by-step guidance that has

helped thousands of parents integrate baby sign language into their daily routine. It's widely known that parents don't have much free time to learn about baby sign language.

This book offers simple strategies to learn the basics of baby sign language that will help you get started.

With this book, your child will quickly learn to communicate about everything that goes on in their little world—and you'll have fun doing it.

Baby indication/sign language is the manual method of putting your signature on a child, connecting with babies and small children's emotions, wishes, and desires via indications, signs, or gesture. Before a child begins to develop his/her speaking ability, with the assistance and encouragement of the parent, expressing something through the movement of the limbs or body is normal, as a result of this, putting a signature on the sensory, developmental part of the child can be referred to as **gesture.**

These types of gestures are also expressed with

emphasized speech to the hearing of kids, but not the same as sign language. Some common benefits which have been discovered by using baby sign language include; a stable parent-child relationship and conversation, minimum disappointments, and improvement on self-esteem for both mother or father and kid. Furthermore, experts discovered that baby sign do not harm the speech building process of babies, the baby rather finds it more attractive as they receive well-passed signals, which makes it essential to inform caregivers about your choice to use baby signals.

Chapter 1

Overview of Sign Language

Kid's sign entails improved actions and modified signals that infants are taught with spoken terms, to truly have a stronger parent-child conversation. The principal reason that parents utilize baby indication/sign continues to be that it'll reduce the aggravation associated with attempting to interpret their unique pre-verbal infant's needs.

Maybe it's considered a fantastic method of a conversation in the first developmental phases since conversation creation employs children's capacity for expressing themselves through physical motion.

Babies' indication/sign is normally distinct. Baby indication/sign is utilized by just hearing parents and hearing children to improve communication. An indication/sign language includes ASL, BSL, ISL as well as organic languages, typically within the deaf community. Indication/sign dialects maintain steadily its syntax and because indication/sign dialects are as natural to understand as every spoken language.

Teaching baby signs permits greater versatility using signs and cannot require the father or mother to comprehend the syntax of the indicator language. Baby indicators tend to be gestures or indicators extracted from your sign language community and altered to be sure they may be easier simply for a kid to create.

Extremely common for the difference between symbolic actions and baby indication/signs among numerous others to be mistaken. Representational gestures certainly are a sort of conversation that kids adopt right before they develop the ability to talk. This consists of aiming from what they want or employing a hand movement as well as a word which allows even more significant conversation for babies.

Babies from about 50 % a year old may begin to understand the fundamental symptoms, which cover such items and ideas as "thirsty", "dairy", "normal water", "starving", "sleepy", "pacifier", "more", "hot", "chilly", "fun", "shower", and "teddy carry". Typically, developing children can produce their unique first actions between your age ranges of 9 months and a year without motivation or assistance from a caregiver. Newborns learn how to utilize their body gestures, vision look, and hands gestures to appeal, showing interest, and connect. Once kids gain several language creations, they'll speak several language having a gesture to greatly help expand connectivity. Movement remains within everyone at any generation, which really is a differentiating factor from baby indication/sign.

Why it could be neither helpful nor dangerous

The procedure for even more assisting gesturing with baby signs is preferred to probably cause disturbance toward kid's mapping of what. This is because of babies lacking enough concentrate on taking both these types of information and process this at exactly the same time. They have advocated these labeling and extra through the facilitation of baby indication/sign, that it is unlikely that baby indication/sign is assisting talk advancement in newborns.

Baby signal programs motivate parents to improve their conversation skills among themselves and their babies before they start experiencing the conversation.

Research proves that children who also participated in baby indication/sign had comparable language advancement to kids who didn't learn baby indication/sign. It's advocated that getting involved in baby indication/sign could be an unneeded use when getting motivated by expectations of advanced language learning designed for the kid.

Nevertheless, it had been found that moms who used baby sign using their newborns motivated increased self-reliance with most of them and backed an increased amount of independence with regards to child. Yet another conducted study shows there are no significant variations discovered with language acquisition among babies who are also obtaining or not getting connection with baby indication/sign, including achieving language breakthrough. Additionally there is zero unwanted effects found out to get in touch with language advancement whenever using an infant sign together with your child. It is possible that baby sign is utilized to get baby's spoken language, but was not found to greatly help expand theirs down the road language advancement.

The final results of multiple studies concerning baby signal can see that advantages supplied usually do not exceed children more than 2 yrs. The results haven't shown support that baby sign raises an infant's linguistic advancement. When teaching an infant indication/sign, an infant's interest is aimed from what they are considering, which is redirected towards adult and the mandatory indication/sign.

This conversation continues to be stated to improve joint attention among father or mother and child, yet must be analyzed enough in research articles. It has also been proposed by just analysts that baby sign may boost parental tension instead of lower it because of busy lifestyles, which might cause disrupting relationships among parents and children.

Achieving fundamental linguistic breakthrough as well as the organic span of kid's language advancement continues to be recommended to become interrupted due to the unnatural solution in language development that baby sign provides, backed with less sustain in prior research that was examined.

Learning baby sign

You'll find a lot of concepts to note when learning baby sign. Caregivers must ensure they possess their baby's attention, preserve regularity knowing what sign could be used and correctly how that is utilized in relation to something, do signs frequently, encourage the newborn, and become alert to recognizing when the newborn is responding with signs.

In relation to newborns which have not yet obtained language capabilities, signs certainly are a simple and easily available type of conversation. Before babies learn particular signs or develop language skills, they'll discover the natural usage of motion. An infant's first motion can occur within 9-12 weeks old.

Gesturing obtain boosted as newborns connect directly to term sign, creating a gesture-plus-word mixture that may develop in to a two-phrase combination. It really is thought that actions could be even more straightforward for babies to keep in mind in comparison with a name just since a gesture is usually a consultant of what a child can picture occurring when considering the item.

To regulate what sort of baby conversation is suffering from touch and talk, Iverson and Goldin-Meadow completed a written report. Babies in the analysis used attention gaze, body position, and vocalization to attract and immediate their unique concentrate on the audience's attention while gesturing to items. Effects seemed to get out if the gestures that children utilize are from the term they say while performing the motion. Iverson and Goldin-Meadow found that newborns move toward goods that they aren't with the capacity of communicating with signs.

Symbolic touch may be the precise term that encompasses baby sign. This sort of motion supports conversation through the use of hands movement that represents something or feeling. Babies are quick to note when there's a link between something and a representational gesture. Once they produce the bond, babies will indeed imitate activities that are created from the caregiver. Regularity through the caregiver is essential through the teaching and opinions stage for newborns to review its repetition.

This repetition concerns what sort of caregiver uses, the sign and in what way the sign could be from the topic or feelings. If the association is adjusted, in that case your kid could have a harder period focusing on the way the symbolic touch links compared to that. One technique for caregivers to ensure the infant affiliates the symbolic motion with finished or feelings is definitely to obtain the baby's attention and say the name of that or situation at exactly the same time that this sign is conducted.

Newborns watch their unique caregiver during everyday routines and circumstances. This statement allows babies to understand signs by imitating the actions in the noticed method. An all-natural relationship happens between indicators and products, allowing newborns to explore and express new ideas right before language advancement. Babies can work out how to correlate a phrase with the entire movement that they perform when working with a subject, such as for example tossing a ball.

Third, relationship, a child starts producing contacts with

the word and move by him or herself, in this case, a tossing motion. Newborns at this time could make the tossing touch to notify caregivers that they wish to toss a ball, thus raising their nonverbal communication. Skills of the kind are further employed by infants showing emotions because they connect a movement or sign with a feeling.

Further research demonstrates that increasing the usage of the motion, not at all use an indicator language can enhance the richness from the child's language development. It's advocated that learning signs occur over an interval, inferring the necessity for caregivers and specific with kids, since it requires more significant interaction between father or mother and child. Parent-child interactions are crucial to working out of baby sign as the baby seems to the caregiver on direction.

Just by consciously showing the sign towards the newborn, the caregiver and baby are preserving joint interest which raises communication.

When caregivers support babies in creating the sign utilizing their hands, they might be further raising encouragement, repetition, and conversation. It is the caregiver's job to never simply train specific hands indicators, and what newborns naturally grab, but to provide support and reactions to babies when symptoms are adequately made. Because they build a relationship, and parental support of the connection, infants may learn and actively be a part of baby sign language.

In 1998, a credit card application was executed at A. Sophie Rogers Infant-Toddler Lab College in Ohio Condition University by Kimberlee Whaley, babies as young as nine weeks and couple of months old and their educators started to work out how to use many symptoms from American Sign Language to speak to each other effectively. The program found that kids would make use of the signs they'll obtain in the classroom in the home. Based on this research, learning baby sign is a helpful tool designed for children if they're applied in classes and daycares.

Press and the web affect

A written report analyzed the quantity of information about the infant sign on the web was based on the analysis.

Results discovered thirty-three websites that advertised baby sign as well as the tremendous benefits associated. A lot more than 90% of the info described opinionated content/articles or promotional items motivating parents to sign language, with small to zero bases in research. Despite the fact that websites declare that using baby sign will reduce tantrums, boost infant's self-pride, satisfaction, emotions of achievement, increase parent-child bonding, and lower disappointment, web sites usually do not provide a lot of research-based proof to assist these kinds of claims.

Researchers investigated whether effects stated for kid have motivational developmental, sociable, cognitive, and language abilities while attaining a larger connection between father or mother and kid. The goal of requesting this query was to find details which allow parents, caregivers, child educators, and clinicians to create informed decisions about the amount of emphasis to put up an infant sign. When all of the reported materials were collected, there were 1747 quite happy with simply ten content providing analysis regarding baby's development bring about connection with an infant sign.

Consensus collected from these kinds of 10 content material says that baby sign, as employed in a commercial sense advertised item authored by Acredolo and Goodwyn, won't advantage the language creation or parent-child associations. However, additionally, there is absolutely no proof from these kinds of articles that baby sign reaches all bad for newborns. Through both these studies, it really is illustrated that websites may not contain research centered information.

People looking for information regarding the huge benefits and drawbacks of using baby sign must ensure these are accessing sites supported by research instead of opinion.

Industrial products available to parents getting involved in baby sign workshops or implementing this in the home are located to be similar to the grade of products within clinical tests. It's advocated that parents keep an eye on baby sign products because it is usually difficult showing the standing of commercialized products simply for facilitating baby sign together with your kid.

Chapter 2

Training Your Baby Sign Language
Starting out

One thing you are able to do before starting to teach your infant sign language is without a doubt selecting the indicators you begin with. I would suggest picking a handful of signs; nearly all parents choose symptoms that have regards to consumption like "eat," "drink," or "take." Toss in a few fun signs like "kitty," "shower," or "sleep," too.

You'll get a chance to find out and choose the signs you utilize to instruct your child sign language within the next stage.

Signing

When you begin to sign, the word is directly before, during, or following an activity. For example, during nursing, sign "drink" or before eating, sign "eat." Continue to show your son or daughter the sign often and stay constant.

Continue using these signs until your son or daughter begins to sign them back. Then, select another sign and begin the task over. Make sure to do not end using the indicators your son or daughter currently knows.

Baby sign language

The greater signs your son or daughter understands, the easier it'll be on her behalf to comprehend them. Your son or daughter may also grab signs quicker as the child learns that he / she could easily get her needs met by just using them.

You don't need to register the surroundings. With infant sign language, you may get the baby's attention by merely placing your signature to finished. you are discussing, and even putting your signs on your own child!

Is Your Son Or Daughter Ready?

At this time that you realize the basics of training your child sign language, I'm absolutely sure you intend to know when to start out! Some parents begin at delivery, even though some do not actually learn about baby sign language until their baby is a year old. There is absolutely no magic involved, and maybe it's hard to learn if your kid is ready.

Whenever your child can sit up just, without needing your help carry himself up, he'll not only proceed through your signs better but also more able to sign backwards. This generally happens between 6 and 9 weeks old.

You will also want to see if your son or daughter is showing a desire to have things you perform using the hands or do in the home. If your son or daughter enjoys watching the family dog or gets thrilled when you work, drink water, or have a shower, he/she often will get some advice about communication. All of them are things your son or daughter would like to sign about, and not just needs, yet also points that motivate her or him.

Probably your son or daughter was already signing. Kids can invent indicators of their own, including directing or mimicking what they've noticed. Family may likewise have trained signs without even recognizing. A fantastic example of that is a youngster learning how exactly to influx "bye-bye" before they can state it. Therefore, your son or daughter was already receptive to signs.

Inspiration

Mealtime has become the logical starting place, whenever your child needs medical assistance, nearly all his attention focuses on meals. That's the reason many parents concentrate on signs that describe consuming and consuming. "Dairy" is normally the most used beginning sign also due to the inspiration of meals; your son or daughter can be hugely receptive. Otherwise, your baby's diet program adjustments and improves, as well as the language of food indicators.

A bathing period can be an additional excellent period for the sign. You will see how your son or daughter reacts to drinking water temperature, try to communicate being dirty, as well as explaining your baby's shower toys. Bedtime is a superb time and energy to sign too; you are able to sign about rest, your baby's blanket or security item, heat, as well as what you notice from the windows.

Chapter 3

Sign Language for Infants
Start Speaking

Are you collecting to begin placing your signature to? That's so thrilling; it's period to get the signs you're likely to start with. Continue and select just a little quantity of symptoms beneath (make sure to bring not merely need-based signs but also signs that may excite your son or daughter as well):

- BATH
- PARROT
- CAT
- DOG
- DRINK
- EAT
- FATHER
- COMPLETE
- FLOWER

- HELP
- HOT
- HARM
- LIGHT
- DAIRY
- MORE
- MOM
- WATER

A substantial thing to bear in mind is to convey the term when you sign everything to your son or daughter, think of placing your signature to as well as putting a focus on your terms if you're talking to your son or daughter. Do not indicate before, during, or after an activity!

What things to remember:

- End up being Excited.
- Do not be bored while signing to your son or daughter, or he or she'll in no way be excited about it!
- Use many signs.
- Don't just sign together with your child in the home.

- Sign in the store, at grandma's house, on the doctor's office, just about everywhere! Signing together with your child brings the very best out of him/her.
- Closing up being Praiseful
- Be content and excited whenever your child signs correctly. Make certain she or he understands how fantastic it really is.
- End up being patient

It requires several infants' weeks or perhaps a couple of months to make their unique first sign. Don't be discouraged; keep placing your signature to and become constant. Your son or daughter would get on the proper track.

Chapter 4

Teach Your Child Sign Language
Caregivers

Some parents who utilize baby sign language stay alert to youngsters although some keep it for function. If you are working abroad, you'll probably leave your son or daughter having a caregiver or relative.

If the baby's caregiver is normally not confusing in signing plan of action, this is of interest for you personally. You may be concerned that your caregiver not placing your signature to together with your child may affect your time and efforts. This is not the situation. If you are signing together with your child, as well as your caregiver isn't, it could hinder working out process, if a caregiver signs together with your child, it really is a substantial addition.

The point is, be particular about your son or daughter placing your signature to together with your caregiver. Explain the huge benefits you can see and suggest to them several indicators. You may be amazed, but many daycares are already applying baby sign language. If yours isn't, you might cause them to become, start using sign language on your own child, and in addition a lot of the additional children. Again, clarify the vast benefits. It will reduce disappointment for the babies, and be great fun as well!

For your babysitter, you should let her/him learn about your signing attempts, teach them several signs that your son or daughter will be much more likely to use. You can provide an indicator/sign language chart for your sitter to use while they're babysitting as well.

Involving family could be considered a satisfying and exciting experience too. Per chance you head to family member's occasions like dinners, birthdays, and vacations. There are excellent times to speak about your baby's signs plus your initiatives; actually, if all your family members obtain educated about your son or daughter new signs; it will always be useful if certainly they know what the signs mean.

Additionally, it's very positive when more folks

understand your sign together with your child. Your infant will feel convenient plus much more likely to become comprehended. There may be some skepticism through the starting though, however in all someone will be impressed whenever your kid shows signs!

Chapter 5

Learn Baby Chat Sign Language
Sign Mixtures

Babies will likely begin to mix vocal phrases (the newborn talk starts!) because they improve of their learning. This is actually the same about placing your signature to kids.

In the event that you sign together with your child long enough, she or he will most likely start merging signs. This may happen in a year, yet will probably occur around 2 yrs. Most youngsters are combining at least two words only at age two. Connecting these signs allows your kid to develop even more fluent conversational skills, and it is breathtaking!

This improvement doesn't necessarily have to be two content; kids chat may continue to contain three, four, as well as five-term mixtures! These combos' help eliminates guesswork.

Some typical common combinations include:

- Color + object.
- "Even more" + yet another sign.
- "Down" + yet another sign.
- Target + "mine".
- "Again" + another sign.
- Person or object + "go."
- "Up" + yet another sign.

Signs and Conversation

Using your kid to be able to combine signs, he or she'll soon learn how to connect signs and voiced words in the same sentence.

Most kids start conversing before they may be done putting your sign-on. You will learn that your kid can replace signs with used words. Your kid will detect spoken terms quickly and use indicators to complete the spaces in his / her voiced language. This might happen even soon after your son or daughter says his / her first phrase.

Children who've faced baby sign language will likely get spoken phrases at an appropriate pace. For the reason that they are already acquainted with the action term, object, or idea, plus they have to exercise their complex, expressive muscles!

Your kid could also continue to use an indicator for any term that individual can currently say. Normally, that is wonderful! or to get the eye (he probably notices precisely how thrilled you get when he signs).

Linking the area

With several combinations, your kid can understand sentences. At this time comes plenty of time when you transfer to more enjoyable and advanced stuff.

When children learn how to speak, they use a conversation pattern that generally includes the keywords within a sentence such as for example; noun, verbs, and several adjectives (that is named Telegraphic Conversation). When you utilize and also have to model entire spoken phrases together with your child, you may utilize the telegraphic talk pattern to get the symptoms you utilize to emphasize your words. When placing your signature to, select the keywords and key phrases to spotlight.

For example, let's feel the phrases: "Feel the bunny! It dropped down." "placing your signature to," your sign could be "rabbit." More technical placing your signature to; includes the sign designed for "down" too.

You truly can expand your child's language in this manner. In the event that you sign several words within a phrase, your son or daughter might have the capability to grab more signs.

Chapter 6

Baby Sign Language Techniques

Toning down Stress

Placing your signature to, as we said before, is fantastic for avoiding tantrums together with your child. Signing help eliminates the aggravation your kid possess if they can't connect.

For instance, whenever your son or daughter is frantically waving her hands in the air and signing "support" for you personally, you should sign "help" back while asking what she or he requires assistance. She'd then try to indicate the word designed "teddy store" you will be trying to teach her or him. You now recognize that he / she really wants to carry the teddy that's too much up to realize. Without placing your signature to, before your kid speaks, you will experience no clue, and she'd have grown to be extremely discouraged.

With sign language, your son or daughter can connect her desires, needs, and feelings with you. There may be no considerably less aggravation when it could be done.

I believe "help" is an extremely most readily useful indicator to use together with your child. While your son or daughter grows, he or she'll need a lot of help with things-reaching things that are too much, opening jugs, working toys, etc. You will make sure to consist of this term within your language.

I also have to make sure to know that despite the fact that placing your signature to aids and relieves stress and produces fewer tantrums, not all tantrums find yourself being prevented. Occasionally, it might appear that putting your sign-on isn't assisting whatsoever. However, it really is difficult to understand how your son or daughter could have taken care of immediately some things without putting your remain. Simply stay confident will be giving your kid the ability to connect, and stay positive!

I would like to take time to indicate the vital signs that I really believe should help your child's putting your signs on. There are simply three, yet I really believe they are crucial and may relieve a whole lot of stress while your kid keeps growing, active, and discovering her environment.

One event that may trigger some tension for your kid comes with an additional baby. Your kid gets disappointed in case your interest with her declines. Make sure to enlist the help of a member from the family during this time period. Having a member of family spend additional time with your child can easily and greatly help when you are unable to stick with him/her.

If you choose to sign together with your newborn, that is very fun for your kid. She'll sometimes be considered a great help out with teaching signs to his / her new sibling and will also relearn the signs she or he discovered when younger. This provides your son or daughter self-confidence and can enhance brotherly bonding in the middle of your two children!

Chapter 7

Train Your Child Sign Language 1
Advancing

Your kid grows and advance! Precisely how fascinating! You are likely combining indicators and conversation together with your child. This would considerably enhance his / her language alongside giving her or him the capability to learn new principles that he/she might possibly not have the capability to explain in words.

There are tons more pleasurable actions you may take now to teach your son or daughter sign language. At this time included in these are: incorporating the ABC, colors, and figures into video gaming and activities.

Whenever your son or daughter is merely about 1.5 years to two years older, you can start teaching her or him the alphabet. You are able to sing a song despite the fact that putting your remain to the characters to begin with. You can even create your child's name and indicate what you display/sign them.

Your kid may be having issues forming the characters due to the fact his / her hands are so little. You should help your kid make up what together with his or her hands. If he will not let you, don't pressure him, he'll eventually catch up.

Colors will also be thrilling; you can start by just teaching her or him the principal colors, then proceed to supplementary, then black, white, red, etc. Indicate colors and sign the colour. Then, check out direct to ensure your kid currently understands the sign for, and attach a color to it. What fun! Once your kid begins to understand colors, your probability of determining what your kid desires will be a lot higher. If your kid demands some things, you are able to inquire what color the truth is, and if they understands the colour, she or he enables you to know!

You may be able to start teaching your kid how exactly to count. Include numbers in to the actions, and make a casino game out of them as well.

As occasions flies, your kid may have perfected all of the signs I'm currently trying to explain to you, get thinking about the signs they understand, or you want to instruct more technical indicators to your son or daughter. Here are some more complex signs that may bring in fresh suggestions and expand your child's world:

- APPLE

- BRUSH-TEETH

- CANDY

- FAMILY MEMBERS

- GRANDFATHER.GRANDMA

- GRAPES

- HOUSE

- WE/ME

- YOUR FAVORITE ICE CREAM

- LION

- MY/MINE

- OFF

- UPON

- OUTSIDE

- PARTY

- PLAY

- Help to make SURE YOU

- SHOES

- CLOTHES

- MANY THANKS

- TIGER

- WOODS

In my own subsequent books, I'll demonstrate how putting your sign-on could be used in combination with your old child and into kindergarten. You're moving along! Thumbs up!

Chapter 8

Advance Toddler Sign Language 2
Your Developing Child

If your kid has began to talk, you may observe that she or he halts using many signs. At the moment, some parents will minimize using sign language because they have obtained what they wanted; a preverbal kind of communication using the youngster. Nevertheless, some parents continue to train the youngster sign language.

There are many advantages from beginning to sign together with your child even after they reach child age. Because your kid begins to combine symptoms and in addition signs with used words, that is a fantastic period to teach her or him even with more indicators. Your son or daughter's language will surely develop, and you'll also transfer to teaching her or him ASL. Your kid will learn things faster due to his / her age. Small kids learn promptly and have the capability to grab second languages quickly at an age-easier than adults!

Actually at age two, most children can discuss 50 words and make two-word combinations. There is without a doubt several variations out of this rule if a kid isn't near these kinds of goals, you should talk to his / her doctor with regards to a possible speech postpone.

You'll find so many methods to keep carefully the signing education together with your kid after she's reached the youngster age:

Walk through the park

This is a sensible way to find out new signs. You are able to indicate an object (a puppy, forest, bird, fencing, etc.) when you walk and present the proper poster. Your children may possibly also request your questions during this time period. What a wise way to produce language!

Read Books

Books are great for your son or daughter's mental development and in addition for learning new signs. Indicate photos, items, and colors, and present the signs to them. You can also start pointing in the characters and providing the ASL indicators for all people as well. This is the starting of reading.

The Zoo

Going to the pet park is amazing whenever your kid can sign. Make sure to have a fresh deal of signs for animals prior to going, though, at least bring along an ASL book and chart!

Parties

Celebrations are exciting places to introduce new signs. You are able to present the signs designed for "cake," "balloon," "gifts," and many more!

They are excellent methods to keep carefully the old child placing your signature to and learning a lot more new languages. These kinds of activities could be games, and they're going to not just exist fun for you personally, also for your son or daughter.

Even if your kid is speaking many words, understanding sign language can be viewed as an excellent advantage. She'll be capable of speaking to the deaf kids in her playgroup, and you will also have the capability to talk with her without saying a phrase. That's a fantastic bonding chance that you ought to possess together with your child.

If you discover out American Sign Language through taking a course or phoning a deaf family member or friend, your kid may learn best along. In the event that you sign together with your kid regularly, they'll certainly detect the signs. Unless you prefer to learn ASL, you are able to sign still as you need to do together with your baby-only placing your signature to particular search phrases. The same as any second language, your kid can grab ASL in the event you have it regularly with family and friends.

Chapter 9

Teaching Infants Sign Language
Obtaining More Signers

Getting associated with additional parents who instruct their infants with sign language can be viewed as a very important thing. Not only are you experiencing some support; nevertheless, you may even produce great friends. When you gather, you can discuss strategies and improvement. You can even learn new indicators, in the event you're placing your signature to friend teaching her kid(s) different signs than you are teaching yours.

Infant's sign language

You are able to choose your playgroup to learn if the other parents are employing sign language using their youngster. When you yourself have teenagers who head to college, you can examine if some of these parents have youngsters and so are using sign language. You might consider a father or mother placing your signature to using the youngster as long as you're in the supermarket or store and may strike up a discussion.

You can also look to placing your signature to playgroups to really get your child (yes, they could be found!) or a course that's targeted on placing your signature to together with your baby, those places certainly are a terrific way to find putting your sign-on parents! If you don't discover a way of putting your sign-on playgroup, you can even begin your own! You can find more parents involved with putting your sign-on utilizing their children and obviously have an enjoyable experience!

Chapter 10

What to Do When Things do not go as Planned

You may encounter several friends or family that doesn't trust placing your signature to your child. Skeptical family and friends will certainly depress your effort.

The misconceptions we alerted you about previously will not imply that placing your signature together with your child won't work. All I could tell you is usually, "wait until your son or daughter starts placing your signature to." They will be amazed and may frequently put their unique skeptic thoughts to relax.

You shouldn't be frightened to state "no" to your son or daughter. Whenever your child learns a fresh word and says the whole day (an indicator you will possibly not constantly need her to possess), you may be frightened to state "No" thinking it might discourage her placing your signature to. This is not true. Your son or daughter will not convert "No" to make reference to her placing your signature to. He or she'll interpret the "No" to make reference to finished. So, don't be frightened. Maintain constant Communication!

Do not focus on your son or daughter's inability to sign backwards. Your child will quickly use your signs over time. He or she'll depend on and could react to your signs, yet might possibly not have the capability to indicate most of them backwards. Infants also work out how to display/sign back differing occasions. Some usually do not present/sign back until after their 1st birthday. Many start placing their signature to at 7 or eight weeks old, yet this differs broadly. Don't get disturbed.

Your baby could also stop placing your signature to suddenly. This may happen as your child may be attempting to execute a physical milestone, which is putting the majority of his / her vigor and desire for it.

Whenever your child starts to sign, the kid may show the same sign designed for different phrases. That's apparent for content like "ball" or "even more" that appear virtually identical. Stay constant, concentrate on the framework, plus your baby will catch up and recognize soon.

Chapter 11

More Signs and Indicators

Shifting from your vital signs you found out in the last sections, here are some supplementary words. They'll branch away a little more from the 1st terms you found and much more cautiously explain the world your son or daughter grows into:

- ONCE AGAIN
- ABC (A-Z) RHYMES
- CARRY
- BOAT
- BOOK
- BREAD
- CAR
- COOKIE
- COW
- DIAPER
- FILTHY

- DOWN
- HIPPO
- FALL-DOWN
- GIRAFFE
- HORSE
- IN
- MONKEY
- AWAY
- TOY
- NEED
- WHERE

You can also decide on a handful of these words in the first handful of signs you choose to start with. Remember; have a look at actions as recommendations; it is not necessary to check out most of them accurately.

Many of these signs may necessitate you to have the hands right into a hand-shape through the manual alphabet. Check the American Sign Language Alphabet website <https://www.startasl.com/american-sign-language-alphabet> or visit <https://bit.ly/2POXriU> to find out these kinds of hand-shapes, their meaning, and many other resourceful info.

These kinds of signs are more technical for your son or daughter. Your son or daughter is typically not capable to perfectly twist his / her hands in to the sign at the moment. Stay constant with placing your signature to the sign correctly, plus your baby's hands will ideal themselves after a while.

Conclusion

Many parents purchase a child sign language DVD AND CD or many books to comprehend what you can see with this precise book in what you have to know before starting baby sign language. You'll want to learn a whole lot already!

Nevertheless, if you undertake the desire for more information than what we've offered, the following we recommend purchasing the ASL chart. A child sign language DVD and Blu-ray are often not cost-free; however, they may be well-crafted and offer different viewpoints and information.

At this time, you have the info and assets to get hold of your child regarding a variety of instances, places, people, wishes, activities, words, actions, colors, and quantities.

You now understand the difference among need-based signs and signs that inspire your kid and possess choosing a small amount of each to teach your baby. If you want to find a lot more indicators to speak about together with your child, you'll get them by checking to get more in online stores.

You additionally have learned to never get frustrated if you are teaching your kid sign language. It could take a while for your kid to obtain it; however when you stay constant, your time and efforts will pay backwards!

You also know how great you should involve your caregivers, family, and good friends in placing your signature to together with your child. It is not only fun nonetheless it is fantastic for your son or daughter to expose to signing in a variety of environments with differing people.

You additionally have found that your kid discovers speech using the Telegraphic Conversation design. Whenever your son or daughter begins combining signs and terms, now you can speak more technical sentences and sign the principal nouns, verbs, and adjectives from the phrases.

You additionally have learned the most simple method of cutting your child's stress by requesting if indeed they want advice about something to allow them to try to indicate what she or he desires, therefore you understand. This may in no way happen in the event that you didn't teach signs!

Additionally, you understand that introducing the alphabet, shapes, and figures whenever your kid is merely about 1.5 years to two years old is obviously possible and intensely fun and educational!

Also, you realize you could continue signing together with your kid also following this individual reaches the youngster age. You can also choose in order to avoid at the moment that you only wished to use sign language for your kid to communicate right before they might talk. You need to use this time to begin with teaching your kid sign language to teach her or him on even more signs to facilitate more spoken phrases.

You additionally have found that placing your signature to other parents can be extremely helpful for both you as well as your child. Additionally, you understand ways to get further information!

Wow! You can see a lot within this book!

This indeed is definitely an exciting period for you personally plus your child. You can see the ultimate way to lessen your child's annoyance, and I'm sure they will be extremely thankful. You took an enormous and caring step designed for your kid, and you need to be extremely happy with yourself!

Of the actions, don't ignore to truly have an excellent time and spend money on your child as much as possible!

Acknowledgments

The Glory of this book success goes to God Almighty and my beautiful Family, Fans, Readers & well-wishers, Customers and Friends for their endless support and encouragements.

www.ingramcontent.com/pod-product-compliance
Lightning Source LLC
Chambersburg PA
CBHW071255070526
44583CB00017B/2474